Sound Advice on

RECORDING
MIXING GUITARS

by Bill Gibson

447 Georgia Street
Vallejo, CA 94590
(707) 554-1935

Publisher: Mike Lawson
Art Director: Stephen Ramirez; Editor: Patrick Runkle
Editorial Assistant: Heather Johnson
PortaStudio 2488 cover image courtesy of Tascam

ProAudio Press is an imprint of artistpro.com, LLC
447 Georgia Street
Vallejo, CA 94590
(707) 554-1935

Also from the ProMusic Press InstantPro Series
Sound Advice on Microphone Techniques
Sound Advice on Compressors, Limiters, Expanders & Gates
Sound Advice on Developing Your Home Studio
Sound Advice on MIDI Production
Sound Advice on Equalizers, Reverbs & Delays
Sound Advice on Mixing

Also from EMBooks
Making the Ultimate Demo, 2nd Ed.
Making Music with Your Computer, 2nd Ed.
Anatomy of a Home Studio

Also from MixBooks
The AudioPro Home Recording Course, Volumes I, II, and III
The Art of Mixing: A Visual Guide to Recording, Engineering, and Production
The Mixing Engineer's Handbook
The Mastering Engineer's Handbook
Music Publishing: The Real Road to Music Business Success, Rev. and Exp. 5th Ed.
Critical Listening and Auditory Perception
Professional Microphone Techniques
Sound for Picture, 2nd Ed.
Music Producers, 2nd Ed.
Live Sound Reinforcement
Professional Sound Reinforcement Techniques
Creative Music Production: Joe Meek's Bold Techniques

Printed in Auburn Hills, MI
ISBN 1-931140-38-3

Contents

Recording and Mixing Guitars

In this book, we cover recording and mixing techniques for four different types of guitar sounds:

- Electric guitars plugged directly into the mixer
- Electric guitars miked at the amplifier
- Electric acoustic guitars, plugged directly into the mixer
- Acoustic guitars recorded with a microphone

Recorded guitar sounds, whether electric or acoustic, can be very dependent on:

- The instrument's condition and intonation
- The technical and artistic ability of the performer
- The microphone used to record the instrument

- The acoustics of the room in which the guitar or amp is recorded
- Choice of dynamic range processing
- Choice of effects processing
- Volume
- EQ
- Panning placement in the mix

We'll evaluate how these important factors influence the recorded sounds of the guitar family. Listen to the Audio Examples several times, thoroughly read all text and practice these techniques in your own setup. It'll make a difference in the sound of your recordings.

Tuning/Instrument Selection

Whenever you record an instrument, your first consideration should be the status of the instrument. Guitar is definitely no exception to this rule. Does it sound good by itself? Are the strings new or old? Is the instrument in tune? Has the intonation of the neck been fine-tuned? Do the notes stay in tune up and down the neck on all strings? Are the electronics within the instrument operating properly?

A guitar with good electronics that's been set up properly has a definite sound advantage over a guitar that has slid away from its peak performance. Correct tuning and intonation give the instrument a wonderful ability to resonate.

Recording Electric

When recording an electric guitar, we have the option of using a microphone at the speaker, running directly into the mixer or combining both of these approaches. Each technique offers advantages and disadvantages. Running direct into the mixer produces ultimate separation. If you process the direct guitar sound, you don't risk altering the sound of another instrument since no other instrument has had the opportunity to bleed into a microphone.

Miking the guitarist's speaker cabinet, although allowing for leakage of another instrument into the guitar mic, typically produces the best sound. Using a microphone on the electric guitarist's cabinet captures the essence of the sound the guitarist designed for the part they're playing. Since sound plays such an important role in what and how a guitarist plays, miking the cabinet is often the only way

Plugging the Guitar Into a Direct Box

1. *Plug the guitar into the direct box.*
2. *Plug the XLR output of direct box into the mic input of the mixer.*
3. *Send the signal to the recorder with the mixer bus assignments.*
4. *Set levels and record.*

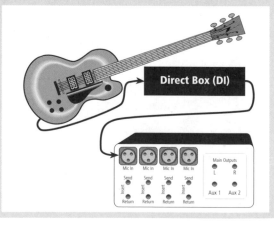

to capture the guitar part in a musically authentic way.

Direct Electric

For the sake of understanding some of the more fundamental variables involved in recording the electric guitar, we'll first plug directly into the mixer. When running a guitar directly into the mic input of a mixer, plug the guitar into a direct box first, then plug the direct box into the mixer. The signal going into the direct box can come straight from the guitar or from any effect or group of effects that the guitar is plugged into. The quality of the DI plays an important role in the sound of the instrument. Direct boxes are available in both passive and active circuitry and the sound quality from device to device varies greatly. If you're a guitarist, find the direct box that gives your guitar the sound you like, buy it, then carry it with you to each recording situation.

Guitar Through Several Effects

1. Plug the guitar into a chain of effects. The output of each effect goes into the input of the next effect.

2. Plug the final effect into a direct box.

3. Connect Out to Amp from the direct box to the input of the guitar amp.

4. Connect the XLR output of the direct box to the XLR microphone input of the mixer.

This setup can be very effective when you need a clean and separate guitar track, but the guitarist prefers to hear from the amp. We can also blend the direct sound with the sound from the microphone for a new and possibly appealing sonic option.

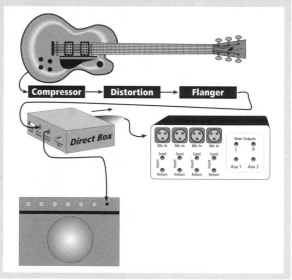

As an alternative, simply plug the guitar straight into the line input of the mixer. This works very well on most modern mixers.

Guitar and Effects to Line Input

1. Plug the guitar directly into the line input of the mixer or plug the guitar into an effects unit.

2. Plug the output of the effects into the line input of the mixer.

The success of this procedure depends largely on the kind of sound you're recording. Distorted, aggressive sounds are best recorded with a mic on the speaker cabinet. Clean guitar sounds with a little compression, chorus and delay often sound very good when run directly into the mixer.

The strength of the signal produced by the guitar is also a factor. Depending on your guitar, mixer and effects, you might experience difficulty getting enough level from the guitar setup to record at 0VU. If you can't get enough level from this configuration, use a DI.

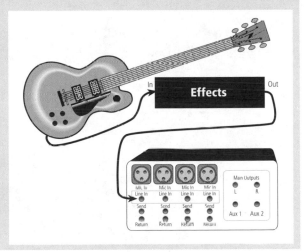

Some guitar amps have a line output. Line Out from a guitar amplifier can be plugged directly into the line input of the mixer. This technique lets you capture some of the amplifier's characteristic

sound while still keeping the advantages of
running direct into the mixer.

Amplifier Line Output to Mixer Line Input

*Some amplifiers have a line output that can be plugged into the line input of
your mixer.*

*This technique can add character to the guitar sound without using a micro-
phone.*

*DANGER! DO NOT PLUG THE GUITAR AMPLIFIER'S SPEAKER OUT-
PUT DIRECTLY INTO LINE INPUT OF THE MIXER!*

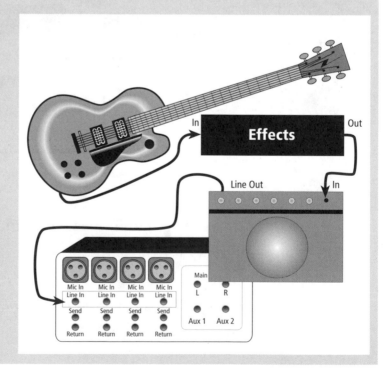

Speaker Output Into a Special Direct Box

BE CAREFUL! *Never plug a powered speaker output into any input you aren't absolutely certain is designed to accept it.*

Some direct boxes have a switched input, letting you select Instrument or Amplifier as the signal source.

This technique can work very well. It adds the characteristic sound of the guitar amp's EQ, distortion and amplifying circuitry without using a microphone.

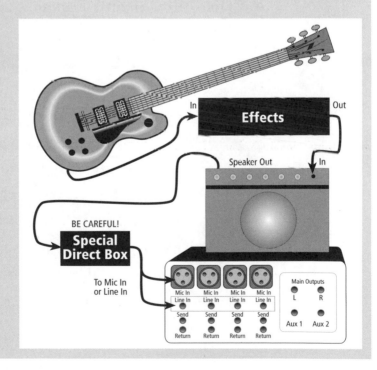

Try using a direct box that will receive a powered signal straight out of the speaker output of the guitar amp. This will give you the most guitar amp sound you can get without using a mic. Be careful!! Never plug a speaker output into any input until you've been assured by someone whose opinion you trust implicitly that the input is designed to accept a powered output!

Advantages of Running Direct

There are 4 main advantages to running directly into the mixer.

1. It's easy. Just plug and play.
2. There's no leakage from other instruments recorded at the same time.
3. It can sound great. With the advent of new guitar effects, the sound can actually be pretty amazing.
4. You can record at home as late as you want without waking the your family, the neighbors, or the police.

Though there's still nothing quite like the sound of a great guitar through a great amp, there are many situations where running direct is more than acceptable.

Analog Levels

When we record guitars, the VU meter should usually read 0VU at the peaks. There can be a couple of exceptions to this rule.

Distorted guitar sounds are often recorded very hot to tape (in the neighborhood of +3 to +5 on the VU meter). Some engineers believe that this adds a little more edge to the part and that the tape being oversaturated has the effect of compressing the sound. This compression helps keep the part in a tighter dynamic range so it can be heard more consistently.

Be careful when recording hot to tape. The signal could become too distorted. You might print so much signal on tape that it begins to spill onto the adjacent tracks as well as onto the track you're trying to record on. The tape recorder and size of tape determine whether or not you can successfully print stronger than normal signals to tape.

Digital Levels

There is no advantage to pushing levels on a digital recording system like your computer work station, hard disk recorder, or MDR. The goal is to simply record the peak level of the track close to or at full digital level. Recording any instrument at unreasonably low digital levels can produce a substandard track that sounds grainy, inaccurate or even noisy.

Transients

If the strings of a guitar are plucked with a hard pick, there are transients in their sound. The extent of the transient depends on the specific instrument, type of guitar pick and the strings. Some acoustic guitar parts contain an exaggerated transient because of the way they've been compressed. Digital meters do a reasonable job of indicating these transients. However, these parts need to be recorded with especially conservative VU levels, in order to compensate for the increased transient attack. Transients have an actual level that is up to 9 dB higher than the VU (average level) reading.

Pickup Types

There are two basic types of guitar: single coil and double coil.

Single coil pickups have a thin, clean and transparent sound, but they can be noisy, picking up occasional radio interference. These pickups, typically found on a stock Fender Stratocaster, are usually about ¾-inch wide and 2½ inches long.

Double coil pickups have a thick, meaty sound and are the most noise-free of the

Single Coil Pickup

This is the approximate size of most single coil pickups. Sometimes they're hidden by a plastic or metal cover. These pickups are common on Fender guitars like the Stratocaster.

Single coil pickups are the most susceptible to noise. If you have a problem with noise when recording a guitar with single coil pickups, try moving the guitarist to a different location in the room. If the noise persists, try having the guitarist face different directions. There's usually somewhere in a 360 degree radius where the noise and interference is minimal. Keep the guitar away from computers, drum machines or other microprocessor-controlled equipment for minimal noise.

Single Coil Pickup

pickup types. They get their name from the fact that they have two single coils working together as one pickup. These are wired together in a way that cancels any noise that is picked up. These can also be called humbucking pickups. Double coil pickups are common on most Gibson guitars like the Les Paul.

Sound Advice on Recording & Mixing Guitars

Many guitars have a combination of single and double coil pickups. It's common for a double coil pickup to have a switch that will turn one of the coils off. This gives the player a choice between single and double coil.

Double Coil Pickup

This pickup configuration uses two single coil pickups working together as one. They're wired together in a way that minimizes noise and radio interference.
Sometimes both pickups are visible, and sometimes they're hidden by a gold, chrome or plastic cover.
The double coil sound is fuller and less shrill than the single coil sound.

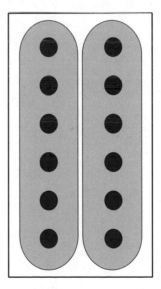

Double Coil Pickup

Compressor/Limiter/Gate/Expander

It's very common to use a compressor on an electric guitar. Most guitars have a very wide dynamic range, and many instruments have uneven string volumes due to sub-standard adjustment of the pickups and string height. A compressor is what gives a guitar that smooth always-in-your-face sound. It puts all the notes and chords into a very narrow dynamic range so there might not be much (if any) volume difference between a lightly plucked single note and a full power chord.

An outboard compressor designed for studio use can do a good job on guitar, but it's normal for the boxes made especially for guitar to work well in a player's setup. Most guitarists use a compressor in their setup, so when recording their guitar sounds, you usually don't need to compress much, if at all. When the guitarist has their stuff together, your job as the recordist is pretty simple. Whether you're running direct in or miking the speaker cabinet, your job is to capture the existing sound accurately rather than creating and shaping a new sound. You can put a compressor on the signal that's coming into the mixer if you need to, but ideally, the guitarist will have a properly adjusted compressor in his kit.

In a guitar setup that uses several effects, the compressor should be the first effect in the chain. This will give the best sounding results and will help guard the rest of the effects from strong signals that might overdrive their inputs.

With a healthy amount of compression, the guitar will sustain longer, plus each note will be audible (even if the guitarist has sloppy technique). Listen to the difference the compressor makes on the simple guitar sounds in Audio Examples 1 and 2. Audio Example 1 was performed and recorded with no compression.

No Compression

Audio Example 2 demonstrates the same part with a healthy amount of compression. I've used a ratio of 4:1 with about 10 dB of gain reduction (refer to Chapter 2 on signal processing if this terminology isn't making sense).

With Compression

Equalization

The recording purist's approach to equalization has always been to record the signal without EQ. It's true that recording with a very extreme EQ can cause problems, but with many guitar sounds, you're endeavoring to create different and unique sounds. The tone is almost always a key ingredient in these sounds so it's usually best to go ahead and print the equalized guitar signal.

A word of caution: If the sound is heavy in bass frequency content, it's generally better to print with less lows than you think you'll need in mixdown. These frequencies are easy to turn up in the mix, and you won't lose anything by saving the addition of lows for mixdown. Low frequencies contain the most energy of all the frequencies and virtually control the VU readings. A sound with too many lows will read unnaturally hot on your meters. If you end up needing more high-frequencies in the mix, they can be buried in the mass of lows. When this happens, your tracks become very noisy. As you try to recover the clarity by boosting the highs, you end up boosting processor noise and tape noise.

Digital Modeling

One of the exciting developments of the digital era is digital modeling. When I plug my Les Paul into my old Fender Deluxe amp, it produces a very characteristic and recognizable sound. That combination not only makes a characteristic sound that

I could recognize a mile away, it also creates a unique and recognizable waveform that can be duplicated and repeated. It's a simple matter of mathematics to calculate the difference between the waveforms of the sound coming directly from the instrument and the sound after it has gone through the amplifier and out the speakers. Once we calculate the difference between the direct and amplified signal, that formula can be applied and added to any direct instrument sound. In this way, sonic character of nearly any amplification system can be cloned with incredible precision and accuracy.

The folks at Line 6 created an amplification system that uses this modeling principal in a very effective way. They have modeled the sounds of many different guitar amplifiers—the original Fenders, Marshalls, Rolands, Hi Watts, and so on. They've also modeled the classic guitar effects, including specific types of compression pedals, delays, choruses, and reverbs. They've even modeled the sound difference between various speaker cabinet configurations, from a single 10-inch speaker to a cabinet with four 12-inch speakers. I've played through most guitar amplification setups and I'm amazed at how accurate these models are. Most guitar effects manufacturers currently offer their own rendition of the modeling system.

Listen to the guitar sounds in Audio Example 3. I have a Gibson Les Paul plugged straight into the Line 6 amp, then running direct into the console. Those who've played guitar through these amps should recognize the sounds as very accurate and authentic. Since the modeling is so accurate, the amplification systems on these units must be clean and sonically transparent enough to faithfully reproduces the modeled sounds.

Audio Example 3
The Fender, the Marshall, the Roland JC-120, and the Hi Watt Sounds

This innovative company also offers The Pod, which has several different amps and effects available along with a software interface for storing effects and creating patches.

MIDI Controlled Instrument Effects

Many effects provide MIDI controlled computer interface applications that let the user have easy access to all parameters. Packages like the one below from the Line 6 POD provide additional features and options within the software domain which aren't available on the actual hardware.

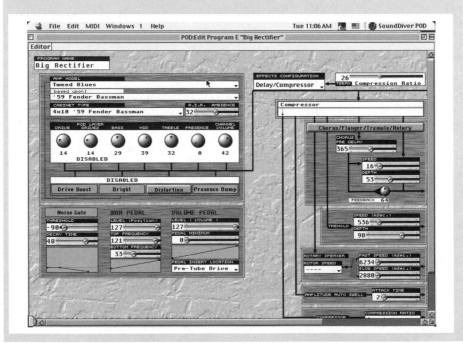

As a purist, one might or might not appreciate the accuracy of these models. There is something special about the sound of the real thing that's difficult to quantify mathematically. However, there's no denying that these modelling systems provide vast flexibility to the home recordist who probably doesn't have all the classic amps and instruments readily available.

Delay

The use of delay on a guitar sound has the effect of placing the sound in a simple acoustical space. Delays of between 250 and 350ms can give a full sound for vocal and instrumental solos (especially on ballads). This is a very popular sound. It's usually most desirable if the delay is in time with the music in some way. Audio Example 4 was recorded at a tempo of 120bpm. I've added a 350ms delay, which is in time with the eighth note at this tempo.

The 350ms Delay

A slapback delay of 62.5ms is in time with the 32nd note, at 120bpm, and gives an entirely different feel to Audio Example 5.

The 62.5ms Delay

Regenerating a longer delay of about 200 to 350ms can really smooth out a part. All of these effects usually make the guitarist sound like a better player than they really are. Guitarists love that! This enhancement can be advantageous to all concerned, but don't overdo the effects or the part will get lost in the mix. It might lose definition and sound like it's far away.

Should I Print Reverb or Delay to Tape?

There are many different effects that a guitarist can show up with, and most of them sound pretty good. It's tempting to go with whatever sound the guitarist has up at the time and record it to tape. This approach can work well and might be preferred if you don't have much processing gear.

Ideally, have the guitarist get a good sound using whatever compression and distortion is needed for the part, but save the addition of all reverbs, delays and choruses for mixdown. Record the raw sound and finish shaping it in the mix. This approach lets you get just the right delay length, delay amount, reverb sound and chorus, after you can hear the part in the context of the rest of the arrangement.

Be flexible. If a guitarist has come up with a great sound that might take you a while to duplicate, and if they want to print the sound to tape, give it a try. Be conservative in the amount of reverb and delay that is included.

There are no hard and fast rules when it comes to creating innovative and exciting new sounds, so be open to trying new tricks.

The Most Common Approach to Miking an Amp

Turn the amp up to a fairly strong level. This doesn't have to be screaming loud, but most amps sound fuller if they're turned up a bit.

Next, place a moving-coil mic about one foot away from the speaker. Most guitar amps will have one or two full range speakers. These speakers are typically 8 to 12 inches in diameter. Moving-coil mics are the preferred choice for close-miking amplifiers because they can handle plenty of volume before they distort the sound. Also, the tone coloration of a moving-coil mic in the higher frequencies can add bite and clarity to the guitar sound.

If the amp you are miking has more than one identical speaker, point the mic at one of the speakers. Point the mic at the center of the speaker to get a sound with more bite and edge. Point the mic more

Sound Advice on Recording & Mixing Guitars

toward the outer rim of the speaker to capture a warmer, smoother sound.

If you're miking a speaker enclosure with separate tweeter, midrange and bass speakers, you'll need to move the mic back two or three feet just to get the overall sound of the cabinet. This gets us into a situation where the room sound becomes an important part of the sound that goes onto the tape.

Audio Example 6 demonstrates the sound of an amp with the mic placed six inches from the speaker and pointed directly at the center of the speaker.

Audio Example 6

Mic at the Center of the Speaker

Audio Example 7 demonstrates the sound of the same amp, same guitar and same musical part as Audio Example 6. Now the mic is aimed about one inch in from the outside rim of the speaker while maintaining the distance of six inches from the speaker.

Audio Example 7
Mic at the Outer Edge of the Speaker

Aiming the Mic at the Speaker

Pointing the mic at the center of the speaker produces a sound with more high-frequency edge.

Pointing the mic away from the center of the speaker and toward the outer edge of the cone produces a warmer, smoother sound with less treble.

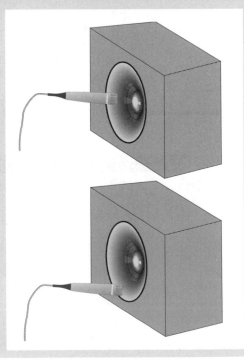

When the mic is within a foot of the speaker, the room sound has minimal effect on the sound that goes to tape, especially if the amp volume is fairly strong. If the guitarist hasn't already included reverb and delay in their selection of effects, this approach will give you consistently close-sounding tracks that you can add distance (ambience) to by adding reverb or delay in the mix.

Powerful guitar sounds often include the sound of the immediate space (the room) that the amp is in. This can be accomplished with reverb, but natural ambience can add an unusual and distinct quality to a recording. Try including the sound of the room with the sound of the guitar. This technique often breathes life into an otherwise dull sound.

As we move the mic back more than a couple of feet from any amp, we're using distant miking. The room sound becomes part of the overall sound. We can get great guitar sounds if we put one mic within a foot of the amp and one mic back in the room several feet away from the amp. With this technique, we can blend the sound of the mic closest to the amp with ambient sound captured by the mic farther away. We can combine these two sounds to one track as we record, or if tracks permit, we can print each mic to a separate track and save the blending or panning for mix-down. The effectiveness of this approach is dependent on whether the sound of the room is musically appropriate.

Use a condenser mic to record the most accurate sound of the room. Condensers have a fuller sound from a distance than moving-coil or ribbon mics and they capture the subtleties of the room sound in more detail. In Audio Example 8, I've placed a condenser mic about seven feet away from the amp.

Audio Example 8
Condenser Mic Seven Feet From the Amp

Audio Example 9 demonstrates the amp in Audio Example 8 through a close mic.

Audio Example 9
Close-miking the Amp

In Audio Example 10, I blend the sound of the close mic with the sound of the distant mic and then pan the two apart.

Audio Example 10
Combining the Close and Distant Mics

Audio Example 11
Multiple-Room Miking

It's often difficult to get that perfectly blended electric guitar sound. Experimentation with microphone techniques can really help solve some problems. The key factors involved in shaping guitar sounds are the raw sound from the instrument, choice of effects and acoustical interaction of the sound in the room. There's much room for creativity here. Start practicing and building your own arsenal of techniques. With the rapid development of affordable technology right now, you'll need to use all available resources to create a new and unique sound that can rise above the masses.

Combining the Miked and Direct Signals

It's possible and common to blend the miked amplifier signal with the direct signal. Plug the guitar into the direct box, then plug into an amplifier from the DIs's out to amp jack. Once this is completed, proceed with miking the amp. From the direct box you can also patch the low-impedance XLR output into the mic input of your mixer. With this setup the direct signal is coming in one channel, and the microphone signal is coming in another channel.

Listen to Audio Example 12. I'll turn up the direct signal alone, then I'll turn the miked signal up alone and finally I'll blend the two sounds and pan them apart.

Audio Example 12
Combining Miked and Direct Signals

Recording Acoustic

Acoustic guitars with pickups can work well in a live performance situation. Simply plug into the board, an amp or through a direct box. You can get a passable sound and eliminate one microphone in the setup. Though the sound is okay for live performances it's hardly ever a great sound for recording. The sound from an

electric acoustic pickup typically sounds
sterile and small and it doesn't have the
broad, full, interesting sound of the
acoustic instrument. To run an electric

Combining the Direct and Miked Sounds

*This technique lets you blend the miked sound with the direct sound. Blend
both of these sounds onto one track or record each to a separate track. Save the
blending for mixdown if possible.*

1. Plug the guitar into the effects.
2. Plug the effects into the Hi Z input of the direct box.
3. Plug the Out to Amp jack into the amplifier input.
4. Plug the Lo Z XLR out-
put of the direct box into the
XLR mic input of the mixer.
5. Mike the speaker, and
connect the mic to a separate
mic input on the mixer.

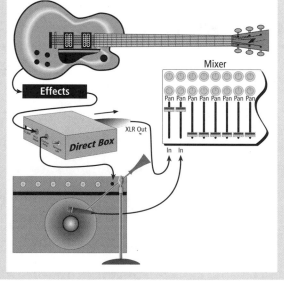

acoustic guitar direct into a mixer, follow the same procedure as with any electric guitar.

The miked guitar has more tone and character; it sounds better. If you don't want the true sound of the instrument, running direct can produce some unique and usable sounds. There are all sorts of variables that can cause us to record in atypical ways. We need to be open to almost any approach in the interest of finding a new and exciting sound.

Dynamic Processing and the Acoustic Guitar

Acoustic guitars have a wide dynamic range. A compressor can help even out the volume level of the different pitch ranges and strings. Some instruments even have individual notes that are much louder than others. Low notes (on the larger strings) will often produce a lot more energy and volume than higher notes on the smaller strings—it all depends on the instrument.

Try this approach to compressing the acoustic guitar:

- Set the ratio control between 3:1 and 5:1.
- Adjust the attack time. Slower attack times accentuate the sound of the pick. The fastest attack times will de-emphasize the sound of the pick.
- Adjust the release time. Setting this control between one and two seconds usually sounds the smoothest.
- Adjust the threshold for a gain reduction of 3 to 7 dB on the loudest part of the track.

Audio Example 13 demonstrates the acoustic guitar without compression.

Audio Example 13

No Compression

One Uncompressed Note on Acoustic Guitar

The encircled area of this graph shows a 5 dB peak from the average level. It represents the attack of the note.

This graph shows a single plucked note on an acoustic guitar without compression. Notice the 5 dB peak on the attack.

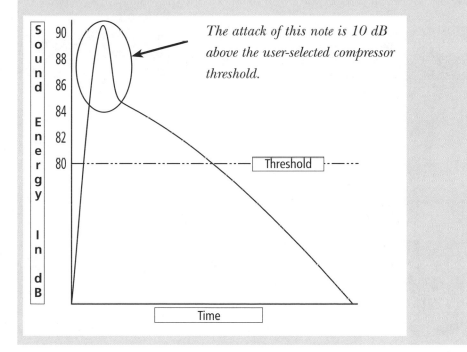

The attack of this note is 10 dB above the user-selected compressor threshold.

Audio Example 14 uses the same acoustic guitar as Audio Example 13. This time the signal is compressed with a gain reduction of up to 7 dB.

Compressed

Compressed Guitar Note With a Fast Attack

The attack time, represented by the dark gray area, is faster than the attack of the note. Therefore, the attack is compressed according to the ratio.

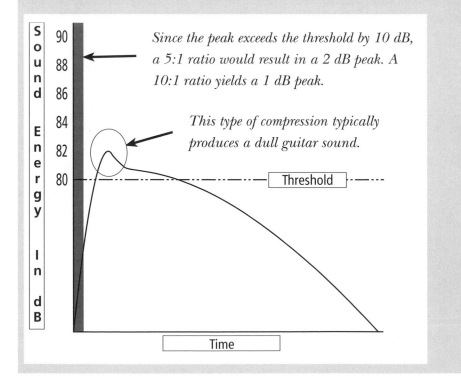

Since the peak exceeds the threshold by 10 dB, a 5:1 ratio would result in a 2 dB peak. A 10:1 ratio yields a 1 dB peak.

This type of compression typically produces a dull guitar sound.

Threshold

Time

Sound Energy In dB

Compressed Guitar Note With a Slow Attack

The attack time is represented by the gray zone. It is set long enough to let the attack of the note pass through uncompressed. Notice the 9 dB peak.

The attack time is longer here than in the previous illustration. Now the attack is not compressed but the rest of the note is. Notice that now the peak is 9 dB above the rest of the note.

All of the note except the attack has been compressed at a ratio of 5:1, so it's only 1 dB over the threshold.

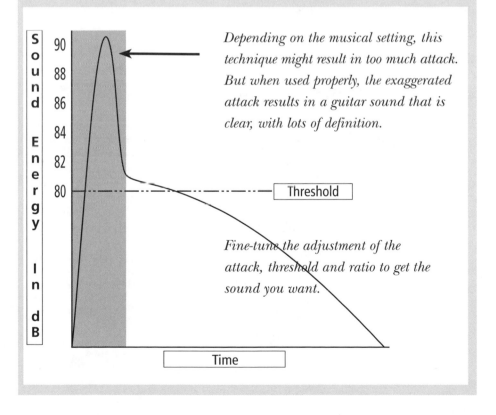

Depending on the musical setting, this technique might result in too much attack. But when used properly, the exaggerated attack results in a guitar sound that is clear, with lots of definition.

Threshold

Fine-tune the adjustment of the attack, threshold and ratio to get the sound you want.

Time

Double Tracking the Acoustic Guitar

One way to get a really full sound from the acoustic is to do a live double track. If you play the original track in the headphones, a good guitarist should be able to duplicate the part with a fair degree of accuracy. Pan these two tracks apart during playback. This creates a chorus-delay-flange-phase shifting effect that happens naturally as the two parts work together.

Audio Examples 15 and 16 demonstrate this double tracking technique. Listen to Audio Example 15 for the original track.

Audio Example 15

Acoustic Guitar

Audio Example 16 shows how adding the double tracked acoustic adds fullness and depth, especially when the two parts are panned away from each other in the stereo spectrum.

Adding the Double Track

Mic Techniques

Typically, the best kind of mic to use on any acoustic guitar is a condenser mic. Condensers capture more of the subtlety of the attack, the sound of the pick on the strings and the nuance of artistic expression. Also, many condenser microphones produce a full sound when miking from a distance. Moving-coil mics and ribbon mics can produce passable acoustic guitar sounds, especially if that's all you have, but the accepted mic of choice for acoustic guitars is a condenser.

Picks

Another very important factor in the sound of an acoustic guitar is the pick. Playing with a thin pick gives a sound that has more clear high frequencies. The thin pick slapping as it plucks the strings becomes part of the sound. Playing with a thick pick produces a full sound with more bass and fewer highs, plus we don't get as much of the pick sound.

Audio Examples 17 and 18 use the same guitar and mic setup. The only change is the guitar pick. Audio Example 17 was performed with a very thin pick.

Audio Example 17

Thin Pick

Audio Example 18 was performed with a very thick pick.

Audio Example 18

Thick Pick

Characteristics of a Good Mix

Strong and Solid, but Controlled, Lows

It's extremely important to build a mix that's distributed evenly in the lows. If the kick is boosted at 100 Hz, the bass should not be boosted at 100 Hz—in fact, most likely the bass should be cut at 100 Hz. Always consider the ramifications of boosting or cutting the same frequency on two or more instruments. If you're limited on your mixer to simple two-band, fixed frequency cut/boost EQ, you must use good mic choice and technique along with educated EQ choices during recording of tracks.

Mids Distributed Evenly Among Various Instruments

Too much midrange results in a "honky" sound. Too few mids results in a hollow, empty sound.

Strong, Smooth Highs That Are Easy to Listen To

A mix that has one particular high frequency boosted on several instruments can take on an abrasive and irritating character. Highs must be distributed evenly.

Balanced

A mix that sounds like it's stronger on one side than the other can be distracting. A good way to check the balance of a mix is on headphones. I'll usually listen to a mix on the phones just before I print the master. Headphones are very telling when it comes to stray instruments that might distract if not placed properly.

Depth

A mix can sound OK if it's two dimensional (just left-right), but when a mix sounds three dimensional—or if the sounds seem distributed from near to far as well as left to right—it becomes much more real sounding. Reverb and delays add depth. It's typically best to have one instrument define the near character and one instrument define the far character. A simple dry percussion instrument is usually a good choice for the closest instrument. A synth string pad or guitar part might be a good choice for the most distant sounding instrument. These choices are all dependent on the desired musical impact.

Width

A stereo mix is more interesting if there is one or two instruments defining the far left and far right boundaries. These boundaries might be far left and far right, but care must be taken to ensure that the mix sounds good in both mono and stereo. Mixes with boundaries closer in toward the center position—3:00 and 9:00 or 10:00 and 2:00—transfer very well to mono, but they aren't as fun to listen to in stereo.

Momentum

If a song maintains the same intensity and texture from start to finish, it probably won't hold the listener's interest. As a mixing engineer, you should always strive to give the song the appropriate flow. That might include starting from just one instrument and the lead vocal and building to a full orchestration with exaggerated effects, or it might include subtle changes throughout the song that are barely noticeable but add enough to maintain the listener's interest.

Consistency

A mix is only good if it sounds good on any system it's played on. Too often a mix will sound really good in the studio or on your own recording setup, but when you play the mix in your car, your living room, the club sound system, the radio or on your friend's mondo home entertainment complex, it sounds embarrassingly bad. Use near-field reference monitors to monitor most of your mix and, as a cross-check, include some larger far-field monitors and some very small radio-like monitors in your setup. Being able to check your mix on two or three sets of speakers can make the difference between good, usable mixes and bad, waste-of-time mixes.

Sounds Good in Stereo and Mono

Continually cross-reference the sound of your mix in stereo and mono. As I've mentioned several times, an instrument, sound or mix can sound great in stereo but terrible in mono. Some of the slight delay or chorus changes that make a mix sound good in mono make practically no difference to the sound of the mix in stereo.

Mixing Electric Guitar

Mixing guitar requires a good understanding of all the effect types along with the technical and artistic skills to incorporate them in a musically inspiring manner. Sometimes, choices are required to eliminate or move ingredients around within the song structure. Technology provides us the tools to mold and shape the arrangement even during mixdown, so a thorough understanding of musical and stylistic considerations is essential.

Doubling

Doubling a guitar part is a very common technique. Doubling can smooth out some of the glitches in the performance and can give the guitar a very wide, bigger-than-life sound. Pan the double apart from the original instrument, and you'll usually get a multidimensional wall of guitar that can sonically carry much of the arrangement. Doubling works well in rock tunes where the guitar must sound very huge and impressive.

This doubling effect can be achieved in a couple of ways. Electronic doubling involves patching the instrument through a short delay, then combining that delay with the original instrument. A live double simply involves playing the part twice onto different tracks or recording two players (playing the identical part) onto one or two tracks. Both techniques sound great. Experiment! Let the music help you decide.

To set up an electronic double, use a delay time between 0ms and about 35ms. Short doubles, below about 7ms, don't give a very broad-sounding double, but they can produce interesting and full sounds and are definitely worth trying. Pan the original guitar to one side and the delay to the other.

Audio Example 19 demonstrates a guitar part doubled electronically using a 23ms delay and no regeneration.

Audio Example 19

The 23ms Double

Audio Example 20 uses the same musical part as Audio Example 19, this time with a live double.

Audio Example 20

The Live Double

Always check a double in mono to make sure the part sounds good in both stereo and mono. Slight changes in delay time can make the part either disappear or cut through strong in mono. Find the delay time that works well in stereo and mono. If you've panned the original full left and the delay full right, the sounds are very impressive in a stereo mix, but these hard-panned tracks often disappear when the mix is played in mono. Try repositioning the pan adjustments so they are only partially left and partially right.

Chorus/Flanger/Phase Shifter

Chorus, flanger and phase-shifting effects are very common and important to most styles of electric guitar. A smooth chorus or flange can give a clean guitar sound a ringing tone. It can add richness that's as inspiring to the rest of the musicians as it is to the guitarist. Listen to the chorus on the clean guitar part in Audio Example 21.

Audio Example 21

Chorus

A smooth phase shifter can add color to a ballad or interest to a funky rhythm guitar comp. Notice the interest that's added to Audio Example 22 by the phase shifter.

Audio Example 22

Phase Shifter

The chorus effects are often part of a solo guitar sound used together with distortion, compression and delay. The guitar in Audio Example 23 is plugged into the compressor first, then the distortion, next the delay and finally the chorus.

Audio Example 23
Multiple Effects

Reverb

Reverb is a useful ingredient in the final mix and is used primarily to smooth out the guitar sound when it must blend into the mix. Too much reverb can spell disaster for the clarity and definition of a good guitar part. On the other hand, reverb can hide many flaws in a marginal guitar part. Adapt to your situation.

Most electric parts sound good with a bright hall reverb sound, a decay time of about 1.5 seconds, a predelay of about 80ms, high diffusion and high density. This kind of setting offers a good place to start in shaping most guitar reverbs. Audio

Example 24 demonstrates a guitar with this set of effects.

Hall Reverb

There are several other types of reverb that can sound great on many different musical parts. Experiment. Often, the sound of the guitar is so interesting with the delay, distortion and chorus that there's really no need for much (if any) reverb. Clean guitar sounds typically benefit the most from interesting and more complex reverb; For instance, slow, open ballads and arena rock projects sound good with hall and chamber reverb using decay times in the range of 1.5–3 seconds. Faster, punchy productions usually work well with plate, inverse and gated reverbs that have a decay time between .5–1.5 seconds.

Try adjusting the predelay to add a different feel to the reverb sound. Longer predelays that match the tempo of the eighth note or quarter note can give both the effect of making the part sound closer to the listener and the effect that it was played in a large room. Listen as I adjust the predelay during Audio Example 25.

Audio Example 25
Adjusting Predelay

Panning

There might be two or more separate guitar parts with totally different sounds in the same song. Though this is common, it can cause a bit of a problem during mix-down where each part should be audible and understandable. Panning can play a key role in helping you separate these different sounding parts for the listener's sake. When used along with different EQ settings for each guitar part, panning the instruments to very specific locations can produce excellent results.

When positioning guitars in the left to right spectrum, be sure that you maintain an even balance for the overall mix. It's common for the guitar to be playing the primary harmonic rhythm part. If that part is panned even slightly to one side the entire mix can sound one-sided.

Sometimes the main guitar part gets in the way of the lead vocal or some other instrument that's panned to center. Rather than panning the two parts apart from each other, try leaving the lead vocal in the center, then running the guitar through an electronic double. Pan the original guitar and the double apart from each other. This keeps the presence and aggressive sound of the guitar but lets the vocal be heard and understood better with less interference from the guitar.

Most modern guitar effects are stereo. They accept the single input from the guitar and have stereo outputs. These stereo outputs usually come from a stereo delay, chorus, flanger or phase shifter that is built into the guitar effects processor. If I have enough available tracks I'll usually print both of those outputs to tape. When there aren't many tracks left you generally can't print both outputs from the effect to tape. This is not really a problem. If we need to we can run the guitar through a stereo chorus, flanger or phase shifter during mixdown.

Conflicting Guitars

A major problem with multiple guitar parts arises when the mix is played in mono. All those tricky panning positions are laid on top of each other as everything goes to the center. It's crucial that each instrument have unique and different EQ characteristics to maintain some identity in a mono mix. The song in Audio Example 26 has three guitar parts. Listen to each part separately and notice that the sound on each is similar. Equalizing like this might sound okay in stereo, but when switched to mono, these parts don't retain much of their identity.

Sound Advice on Recording & Mixing Guitars

In Audio Example 27, first you hear each guitar part separately. Notice that they each have very different sounding EQ. I'll pan them to acceptable positions in the mix. Finally, see if you can still hear all the parts when I switch to mono at the end of the example.

Equalized for Mono

Equalizing the Electric Guitar

There are certain EQ ranges that add specific qualities to guitar sounds. Depending on the type of guitar and style of music, EQ changes can have varying results. Here are some good starting points for equalizing a guitar.

100 Hz can add a good solid low end to most guitar sounds. Boost this frequency sparingly. It can be appropriate to turn this frequency up, but most of the time a boost here will conflict with the bass guitar. I end up cutting this frequency quite often

on guitar. Listen as I turn 100 Hz up and down on the guitar sound in Audio Example 28.

Audio Example 28

Boost and Cut 100 Hz

200 Hz tends to be the muddy zone on many guitar sounds. A boost here can make the overall sound of the guitar dull. A cut at 200 Hz can expose the lows and the highs so that the entire sound has more clarity and low end punch. Cutting this frequency can help a double coil pickup sound like a single coil pickup. Audio Example 29 shows the effect of cutting and boosting 200 Hz.

Audio Example 29

Boost and Cut 200 Hz

The frequency range from 250 Hz to 350 Hz can add punch and help the blend of a distorted rock sound. Notice the change in texture of Audio Example 30 as I boost and cut 300 Hz.

Sound Advice on Recording & Mixing Guitars

Boost and Cut 300 Hz

The frequency range from 500 to 600 Hz often contains most of the body and punchy character. Try to hear the body of the sound change as I cut and boost 550 Hz on the guitar in Audio Example 31.

Boost and Cut 550 Hz

The frequency range from 2.5 kHz to about 5 kHz adds edge and definition to most guitar sounds. I'll boost and cut 4 kHz on the guitar sound in Audio Example 32.

Boost and Cut 4 kHz

Boosting 8 kHz to around 12 kHz makes many guitar sounds shimmer or sparkle. These frequencies can also contain much of the noise from the signal processors so cutting these frequencies slightly can minimize many noise problems from the guitarist's equipment. Listen as I boost and cut 10 kHz on the guitar sound in Audio Example 33.

Audio Example 33
Boost and Cut 10 kHz

Mixing Acoustic Guitar

Equalizing the Acoustic Guitar

We use equalization on acoustic guitar to shape the sound for the space in the mix that we want the guitar to fill. From our audio examples, you can tell that much of the sound can be shaped through mic placement, string selection and pick selection. If we have a well-maintained guitar with the correct mic placed precisely where it should be and a great player playing the appropriate strings with the perfect pick, using impeccable technique to play wonderful parts that have phenomenal artistic expression, we might not need to use much EQ, if any.

Let's look at some common solutions to equalization problems you might encounter when recording acoustic guitars.

The most common equalization of the acoustic guitar involves cutting the low frequencies, below 150 Hz. Lows can be very predominate and boomy on an acoustic guitar. These low frequencies can clash with the bass guitar, bass drum, piano or any full-range instrument. In Audio Example 34, I'll turn the frequencies below 150 Hz down. This can make the guitar sound a little thin when the guitar is by itself, but this sound generally works best in the mix.

Audio Example 34
Cut 150 Hz

Another common EQ for acoustic guitar involves adding a high-frequency shimmer at about 10 to 12 kHz. On the guitar in Audio Example 35, I'll boost 12 kHz.

Boost 12 kHz

If the guitar is sounding muddy, we can usually clean the sound up by turning the lower mids down (between 200 and 500 Hz). Listen to the change in the guitar sound in Audio Example 36 as I turn down the curve centered on 300 Hz.

Cut 300 Hz

When you need more edge or definition from the sound, boost a frequency between 3 and 5 kHz. Audio Example 37 demonstrates the sound of boosting the acoustic guitar at 4 kHz.

Adjust a frequency between 1.5 and 2.5 kHz to emphasize or de-emphasize the sound of the pick hitting the strings. The actual frequency you select depends on the type of strings, gauge of strings, the physical makeup of the guitar and the pick. In Audio Example 38, I boost then cut 2 kHz.

Reverb

The choice of reverberation when recording acoustic guitar is dependent on the musical style and arrangement of the song. In folk, country or blues, the acoustic guitar might use little or no reverb. Any reverberation used in these styles is typically very natural sounding. Hall and chamber settings on digital reverbs can smooth out the sound without being intrusive or obvious. Decay times of one to two seconds work very well. These reverberation settings can help the part blend into the mix without dominating the sound of a song.

On the folk style part in Audio Example 39, I start with no reverberation, then I add a small amount of chamber reverb with a 1.5 second decay time.

Audio Example 39
Chamber Reverb

Pop and commercial rock musical styles are more likely to use chorus type effects and unnatural sounding reverb. Even in these styles, the acoustic guitar is often treated as a natural instrument. If chorus effects or delays are used, they're typically intended to simulate the effect of double tracking.

Ballads are more likely to use more effect on the acoustic guitar. The rich texture of the reverberated guitar can be heard and appreciated in the open texture of a pop ballad.

In the proper context, any of the chorus, flanger or phase shifter effects can sound great on acoustic guitar. The guitar in Audio Example 40 has a stereo flanger and slapback delay set to the same speed as the eighth note. This is a very usable sound, although it doesn't reflect the purist's approach to the acoustic guitar.

Audio Example 40
Flange With Delay

Keyboards and Guitars

It's standard to pan the basic keyboard and guitar apart in the mix. Often, these parts work well when panned to about 3:00 and 9:00, as they are in Audio Example 41.

Keyboard and Guitar Panned Apart

Since it's typical that the guitar and keys have been recorded with effects, there's often not much to do to get these parts to sound rich and full. If you've followed this course from the beginning, you should know several techniques to help shape the sounds of these instruments.

If there's just one basic chord comping part, it's often desirable to create a stereo sound through the use of a delay, chorus or reverb.

Filling Holes With the Guitar or Keys

There's often one instrument that provides the bed—or constant pad—for the song, and another instrument that's a little less constant that can be used to fill some of the holes that might crop up.

This might be one case where the mixing engineer becomes the musical arranger. It could be best if an instrument is only included during certain sections of a song, even though the instrument was recorded throughout the entire song. The process of mixing involves musical decisions.

Deciding exactly what needs to be where is one of the most important parts of the final mix. If too many things are going on at once during a song, the listener can't effectively focus on anything. Frequently, during a session, the basic tracks will be very exciting and punchy, and everyone in the studio can feel the excitement and energy. Eventually, as more and more parts are added, everyone can feel that the music's punch and energy have been buried in a sea of well-intended musical fluff. That's not very exciting.

The old standby rule of thumb continues to pertain in music: Keep it simple.

The more musical parts you include, the harder it is to hear the music.

On this song, we have a keyboard comping part and an acoustic guitar comping part. I recorded both parts all the way through the song, even though it'd probably be cleaner if there were only one of these parts going on at a time. Now that we're mixing, I'll listen to this mix and decide which part should be playing when. There might be a spot toward the end where both should be playing. Listen for yourself. Audio Example 42 demonstrates the rhythm section and vocals with both the guitar and keys comping. Notice how they sometimes work well together but that often they get in each other's way.

Audio Example 42
Mix With Guitar and Keys

Audio Example 43 demonstrates the song with just the keys comping. I've removed the guitar so that the keys can be stronger and punchier in the mix without detracting from the rest of the orchestration.

Audio Example 43

Keys Comping

Audio Example 44 demonstrates the song with just the guitar comping. I've removed the keys so that the guitar can be stronger and punchier in the mix without detracting from the rest of the orchestration.

Audio Example 44

Guitar Comping

For the sake of comparison, listen to all three mix versions edited in a row. Notice the difference in space, feel and emotion as one version transitions to the next.

Audio Example 45

Mix Comparison

Lead Parts—Pick and Choose

It's common to include a lead instrument part; this is typically a guitar, keyboard or sax. It often runs throughout the song filling holes and, essentially, adding spice and emotion while maintaining flow and interest. If you can get the player to play only what's needed on the lead track, your mixing job is easier. Often, when the lead parts are recorded, the total scope of the song, arrangement or orchestration hasn't been defined. In this case, I'll let the lead player fill all the holes he wants, then pick and choose what to include in the mix. If you let the lead part fill all holes between the lyrics, verses or choruses, the element of surprise or contrast is lost. There's an art to finding the appropriate spots to include the lead licks; but remember, at any point of the song there only needs to be one focal point.

Lead parts are usually good to include in the intro, leading into a chorus, between verses and choruses, sometimes between lyric lines and in the repeat choruses at the end of the song.

The modern digital workstation provides flexibility and musical arrangement choices up to the completion of mixdown. Often, the reason a part is difficult to mix is because it's just in the wrong place. Be conscious of the arrangement and use your tools to craft the musical structure in a way that facilitates a great sounding mix.

In the song we're using in this chapter, there's an acoustic rhythm guitar, a simple electric lead part and a solo guitar part. Different songs and styles demand different instrumentation. The electric guitar part here is used to fill throughout the song. A part like this can be turned on and off as needed or you can just let it fly through the entire song. This part provides a focal point between the lyric lines. Listen to the song without the electric part, in Audio Example 46, and notice that the holes between the lyrics lack focus.

Audio Example 46

No Electric Guitar

Audio Example 47 demonstrates the same part of the song, but now I'll include the electric fills. Notice how this maintains interest and helps the flow of the song.

Audio Example 47

With Electric Guitar

The solo part is used for contrast in the intro, at the solo section and in the end during the repeat and fade section. Listen to the intro without the guitar solo part in Audio Example 48.

Audio Example 48

Intro Without Solo

When the solo is included in the intro, it helps give a focal point and define the style and emotion of the song.

Intro With Solo

As a note on solos, keep in mind that it's often good to put the same effects on the solo as the lead vocal. This adds continuity to the emotional flow and acoustical space of the song. Solos are almost always panned center to help keep the focus.

Blend the Sounds

Any mixdown requires careful blending and crafting of each component. To expect that the sounds will simply work together without shaping is unrealistic. Learn the sonic personality of the various EQ frequencies. Intentionally fill certain areas of the bandwidth. At the same time, clear out frequency ranges to make room for other important material.

Every sound in a mix cannot be full-range. Guitar, especially, tempts us. Since the young guitarist spends a lot of time making up patches that sound great at home, all alone, you'll often face a wall of guitar. With such huge guitar sounds there's really no need for other instruments. Once the power of the mix unfolds, as you shape and mold the tracks, you and those around you will be amazed at the difference in the overall sound.

Whether your sounds are clean and pristine or raunchy and dirty, practice the techniques contained in this book and you'll soon see your mixes jump to a new level of power and excitement.